Amazing Nature

This book belongs to

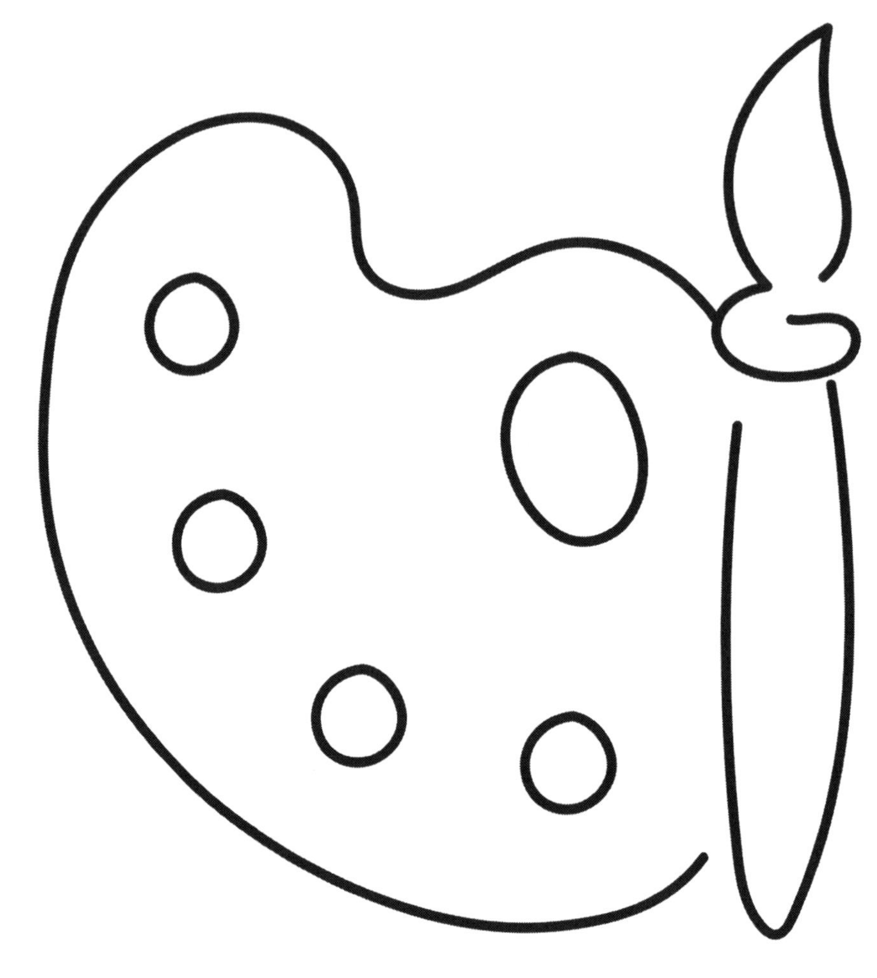

Test your Colors

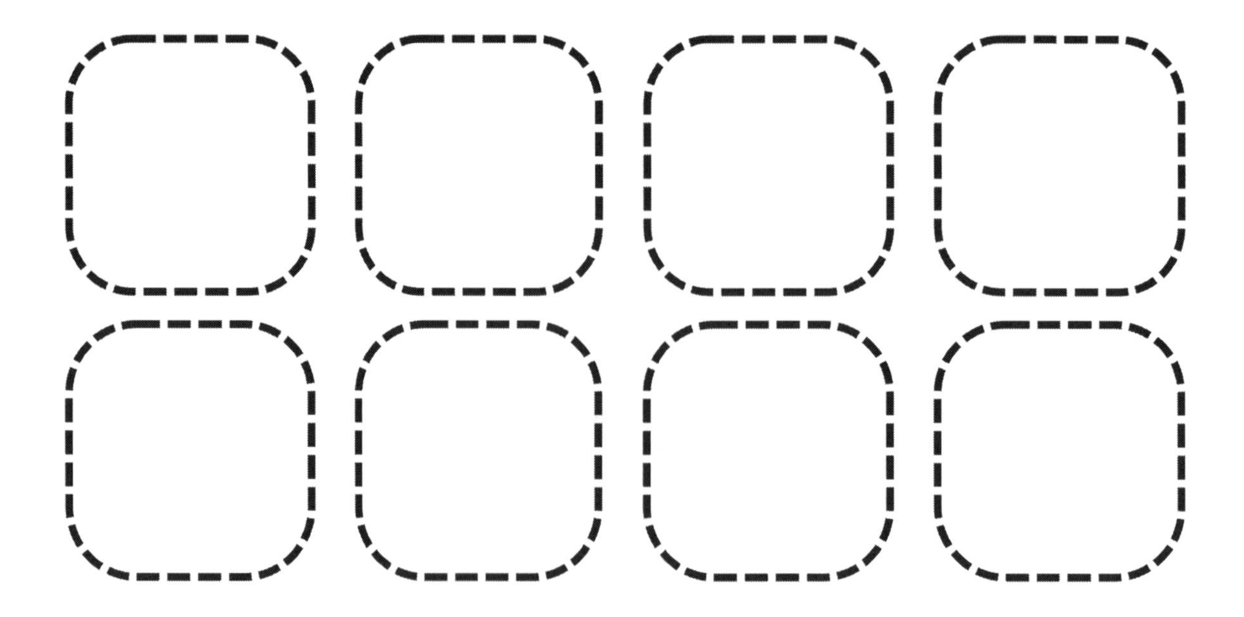

Thank You
please leave a review
or write email :-)

Contact : amz@tafs.shop

Imprint
Tafs Malbucher
Frank Sydow
Richard-Wagner-Str1
38350 Helmstedt

Made in United States
Troutdale, OR
01/07/2024